# HOME SERIES
## DETAILS IN ARCHITECTURE

BETA-PLUS

# CONTENTS

**P. 4-5**
A bathroom designed by
architect Annik Dierckx in a low
energy home.

**P. 6**
The attention to details is of the
highest importance in this
hallway created by architect
Bruno Vanbesien.

## INTRODUCTION

his new volume in our HOME SERIES shows a collection of new projects by architects and interior designers in which their attention to details is of the highest importance.

True mastership is shown in architectural details; the best lighting, handmade doorhandles, beautiful fireplaces, extraordinary staircases, creative use of colours and textures ...   all add the true finishing touch to an interior project.

**P. 8**
One of the bedrooms in the same house as on page 6, a Bruno Vanbesien project.

**P. 10-11**
This hearth is completely finished in a smoked oak veneer. A project by architect Nico Verheyden.

# TRADITIONAL CRAFTSMANSHIP

## IN THE TINIEST DETAIL

D auby is an exclusive importer and wholesaler in various Italian, French and Spanish manufacturers who feel strongly about traditional craftsmanship.

This Antwerp company has existed for thirty years and from its beginnings specialised in top quality door, window and furniture fittings in various styles: from traditional rustic to resolutely contemporary.

The Dauby collections include an extensive range of design models for modern homes but also stylish and timeless door fittings for parsonage, manor and cottage styles. The fittings may be from solid brass, solid bronze, traditional cast iron or exclusive Britannium (a metal alloy including silver and tin).

Interior decoration for this home: Pompadour.

Each door and window handle is completely finished off and given patina by hand.
Through natural corrosion the solid bronze develops a brown oxidation layer and is protected against further corrosion by a layer of bees' wax. The surface is given a lively colour with intensive use; with frequent use the object will become lighter in some places, with less frequent use it will become darker again. The older, the more authentic the fittings become.
Bottom left photo: the range is concerned with the tiniest details, even the doorstop is made from solid bronze.

Dauby's "Pure"-line was created from a few tight models, inspired by the Bauhaus period. These are creations from the early Avant-Garde that testify to a period when the term "design" was still in its infancy.

Each product is carefully cast in sand mould, a traditional English method that dates from the Tartessian period (c. 3000 years BC).

The discrete form of these highly user-friendly kitchen handles honours the straight lined character of the furniture.

Fama only uses bronze, an alloy of copper and tin. Adding tin makes the material harder and less bendable than copper. For instance, the majority of church bells and lots of statues are made from bronze.

Each room has its own decorative touch: with series like Giara, Genifer, Fama and Pure, Dauby always creates a unique environment.

The furniture fittings by Giara are made from Britannium metal (an alloy including silver and tin). When used, a patina develops that gives the material an authentic look: the weathered look is the product's charm.

The straight lines of the Fama door fittings allude to the 1920s and to Art Deco style.

The fittings by Pure are available both in white bronze and in weathered iron.
The white bronze of the Pure-range is an alloy of various non-ferrous metals. The mould sand leaves a rather grainy "skin" after the casting, which gives each piece a unique cachet. The benefit of white bronze: this alloy has an original colour in itself. It does not oxidise and therefore varnishing is not necessary.

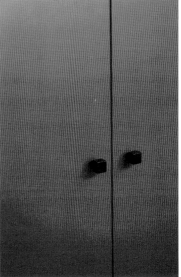

The weathered iron that is processed in the Pure-line is cast iron, cast in sand moulds that are then fully manually finished. The roughness of the form, which is the result of this method, makes a cast iron object immediately identifiable as such. The weathered look is realised by applying a natural dark bees' wax that also protects the iron against corrosion.

Pure has also included lever handles made from white bronze or weathered iron according to choice. This handle fits perfectly with the chosen door, window and furniture fittings. A Ludo Dierckx project.

The original method of sand casting is still used for the manufacture of all Pure-collection pieces.
This gives the Pure-range an authentic and particularly timeless character, which distinguishes them from everyday mass produced items. Each item is produced with love for the craft and is given a natural and increasingly more beautiful patina over time. The older it is, the more valuable the product will appear. A Ludo Dierckx project.

# PASSIONATE ABOUT DETAILS

nterior architect Filip Vanryckeghem is passionate about
details.

The three recent projects from his
design office iXtra show how attention to
detail can enhance the quality and the
comfort of the living spaces.

The existing hearth was retained: it
formed the start of the pattern in this
interior.
The zenithal overhead light – via the
skylight – is a thankful supplement to
the lateral side light via the high
window partition.
The additional artificial light (Diapason
cover from Kreon) is integrated in the
acoustic suspended ceiling via a type of
light duct.

The open living kitchen, with extendible dining table via an invisible sliding section, offers space for a maximum of ten persons.
Integrated base lighting in the wall and ceiling and specific Kreon construction fittings that ensure for a few light accents above the washing up and dining zone. Light profile: Kreon / Prologe 80 on-regule.

The bedroom, with two symmetrically
set-up, sliding dressing room walls.
This room connects directly to the
entrance hall and the bathroom but can
be closed off by the sliding partition.
Integrated ceiling spotlights from Kreon
(Down in-Line 76).

The bathroom is behind the bedroom and forms a single whole. The suspended mirror cupboard with storage function and as a partition between the bath and shower zone includes an integrated TL-fitting at the bottom that fulfills the safety conditions (IP44 for wet rooms). Shower, bath and hand basin were assembled ingeniously by Filip Vanryckeghem into a harmonious and functional whole. Various types of lights ensure a varied atmosphere: a TL-mirror cupboard, shower spotlights from Kreon (Down in-Line 76 with glass sealing (IP44-standard). The Small Diapason wall spots with shadow cap are also from Kreon. TL-lighting of the Lumco type, with separate ballast.

Interior architect Filip Vanryckeghem transformed
an existing, rather monumental extension into a full,
pleasant living space.
In consultation with the customers the decision was
taken to create a restrained, intimate atmosphere.
The large space was consequently also divided,
however without losing the larger cohesion.
The consistent general use of materials for each
space contributed to the coherence and conviviality
of this home environment.

This bathroom set forms a part of a renovation project in a bungalow designed by the architect A. Deheyter.

The elementary functions of the space (hand basin, bath, shower, sauna) were filled well but simultaneously an extra dimension was also striven for: a project that exudes wellness. The skylight above the bath from Kos provides extra atmosphere both during the day and in the evening. The texture of the coarse walls in natural stone creates additional play with light and shade.

In addition to the zenithal light there is also positive lateral daylight, consciously obtained by opening the closed side façade over the entire width and height of the bathroom. In the bathroom niche, integrated at the top: Kreon fittings, Side in-Line.

The same type of Kreon Down in-Line 76 was opted for as general lighting (with glass in the shower in relation to the IP44-standard).

In the sauna room: a coloured TL-strip.

# A HOUSE IN THE LUXEMBOURG

## COUNTRYSIDE

T his house was built in 2007 and is situated in the Luxembourg countryside.

The interior combines both neutral and timeless elements with some antiques, using natural and noble materials.

The house is also used as a show-room for the owners' interior design and decoration business: In Tempo by Luc Leroi. Their philosophy lies in the creation of timeless interiors favouring materials such as natural wood, stone, lime, linen and an overarching use of artisanal work.

The modest entrance hall is laid with church tiles by Dominique Desimpel.

**P.39-41**
The ground floor is laid with antique Corvelyn parquet. The oak chest of drawers is simply stripped. Bespoke armchairs are upholstered in C&C Milano covers.
A sofa upholstered in Libeco linen, a table de vigneron dressed with antique olive wood mortars. All the walls of the lounge and dining room are rendered in Corical lime-wash paint.

A view along the hall affords a full appreciation of the double exposure of the rooms in succession. Curtains in Leitner linen. An antique 19th century chandelier. An 18th century Namur wardrobe holding a collection of Chinese pots.

The kitchen is in untreated oak, with a work top in blue stone and credenza covered in red zellige tiles from Dominique Desimpel. Integrated storage cabinet and fridge in a cupboard painted the same colour as the wall.

The storage units in this pantry have been custom-made. Underfoot, checkerboard flooring in Italian marble by Dominique Desimpel.

The hall leading to the bedrooms is in rough grey oak. A Spanish console table in walnut from the 18th century. C&C Milano linen blinds.

The office has an antique pine table
and an 18th century "Os de mouton"
chair.  Lighting from S.Davidts.

The master bedroom has been rendered in white lime-wash paint. An Anker bedding bed with Libeco linen cover. Wall-lights from Galerie des lampes – Paris.

The bathroom has a monastic feel, in oak, blue-stone and Indian schist tiles. Nautic wall-lights.

This floor is set aside as guest suite. A pine wardrobe originally from the Pyrenees. A Louis XIII banquette upholstered in white *de le Cuona* linen and a coffee table made from a walnut panel supported on a trestle.

# A SPECIAL METAMORPHOSIS

T he commission for interior architect Frederic Kielemoes consisted of creating a cosy atmosphere in a contemporary home with 5.5 m high south facing glass segments.

The original straight staircase was replaced by a lower pitch stair that starts in front of the window frame by means of a plinth in flamed bluestone from Hainaut.

The self-supporting steps are in stained oak, lit with LEDs.
PUK4 type lamp, varnished black, from the Delta Light collection.
The walls are covered in dark stained oak with integrated black varnished aluminium banister.

The 2.7 m long gas hearth with steel, black lacquered plinth was produced by Metalfire.
A Chantecaille reading light in black epoxy from Christian Liaigre.

The dining and living room table were made from stained oak, according to a design by the interior architect Frederic Kielemoes.
The floor is in flamed bluestone.

The incidence of light in the office space is filtered through a curtain of horizontal wooden slats.
All the furniture in dark stained oak with integrated T5-lighting.
Ceiling lighting of the Carree type from Delta Light.

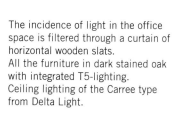

Savannah Blue is a special natural stone with a lot of shades.
With this floor as the base the interior architect Frederic Kielemoes created a design where all the colours were repeated in the interior design and the selection of furniture.
An office is concealed behind the curved wall, which starts from the hall.
This wall has been painted in a dark, graphite colour and ensures depth from the living area.
The low position of the wall lighting (type Max from Delta Light) acts on the dark wall as accent lighting.
All the custom-made work was realised in oak and MDF, and varnished in a graphite colour.
The table (260x100 cm) of lacquered oak is Frederic Kielemoes' own design.

A hand basin in Buxy gris with a work surface and rear wall in brushed oak lacquered graphite. Recessed T5-lighting on the work surface and ceiling lighting of the Carre type from Deltalight.

# HAUTE COUTURE

## IN NATURAL STONE

S tone company Van den Weghe (The Stonecompany) has been one of the leading experts in exclusive custom-made pieces for renowned architects, interior designers and private patrons both nationally and internationally for decades.

The owner and company manager Philippe Van den Weghe combines a fine nose for the newest architectural and interior trends to thorough know-how and a passion for his craft.

Uncompromisingly he searches for the best quality natural stone and finish: the stonecutters and installers from The Stonecompany are amongst the very best in their sector.

"Haute couture": is no hollow slogan for Van den Weghe. Each handmade detail shows the sense of perfection and the passionate know-how of this unique natural stone company.
The new showroom is convincing proof of that.
The counter is made from open book Bianco Statuario marble and fully mitred assembled false solid. The Floor is in large custom-made Basaltina.
The central panel (on the left in the background) is made from wild agate, a semi-precious stone.

The meeting room has a floor in French Sainte Anne stone bordered with Belgian Noir de Mazy. Also pay attention to the detailing on the radiator panel.
The table is made from Bianco Zeus composite stone.

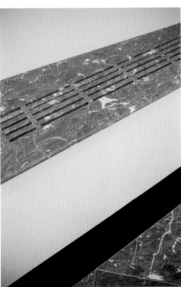

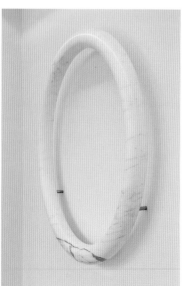

The entrance: the ring and hanging light are made from solid Bianco Statuario.

The walls in the reception office are clad in Bardiglio, with a "Rigato" finish. The same stone is used as an inlay with Lasa marble and Basaltina for the small meeting room. This marquetry is ground smooth on site according to the Italian method. The table is in white Lasa marble.

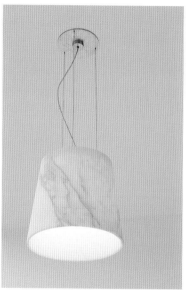

These lights are made from semi-transparent marbles.

The ladies' toilet is finished in Lasa marble with a solid cut hand-basin.
The gentleman's toilet in smokey black, with a false solid assembled hand-basin.

The bathroom is clad in smooth grey quartzite Grigio Luna burned mat and rough for the floor. A design in cooperation with Buro I.

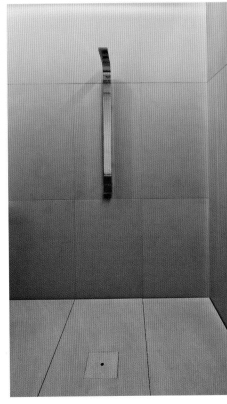

# COMING HOME

W henever living is experienced as "coming home", the desire grows to have each room tastefully come into its own.

Frank Tack has again allowed his know-how to speak, to tastefully design the interior of this manor house, designed by the architect Bernard De Clerck, into a harmonious whole.

The sober, rustic style is translated in an enthusiastic way in this philosophy of living. Each lovingly created piece of furniture by Frank Tack according to the traditional craft exudes this atmosphere. The customised handmade craft, integrated in a refined way in the whole, offers a top quality look in this exceptional realisation.

The exclusive, durable wood exudes class and comfort. The harmonious interplay of noble materials predominates: a passion for perfection and top quality craftsmanship.

All new technological gadgets were concealed behind the traditionally crafted furniture. Every detail contributes to the balance of the proportions in this home.

The sober, rustic custom-made elements make for a stately, spatial look.

The weathered door and furniture fittings contribute to the sober, intimate atmosphere in this living kitchen.
Functionality is purposefully linked to beauty.
The kitchen unmistakably bears Frank Tack's "handmade" signature.

Symbiosis of bleached French oak and the kitchen sink unit in bluestone.

Passionate custom-made work, with a sense of proportion interwoven in a timeless living environment. It shows a feel for refinement and the identity of the inhabitants.
Each room is connected harmoniously through the uniqueness of the furniture wood. Here there is also a striving for perfection in the tiniest detail: the door, furniture and window fittings are perfectly integrated.

The playfulness of each door element reflects the warm unique character of French oak.

A special sample of the craftsmanship of Frank Tack.

# HANDMADE CRAFTSMANSHIP

## AS A GUIDING PRINCIPLE

I n this report on the stone company Van den Weghe – The Stonecompany a few recent projects are shown with hand-made craftsmanship and a passion for details as guiding principles: perfection in custom-made stone as a result of over thirty years' experience in the top segment.

Kitchen work surfaces in bleached Rose Aurore marble with a massive hewn sink.
All design and furniture: Joris Van Apers.

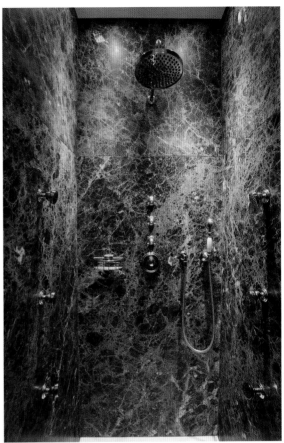

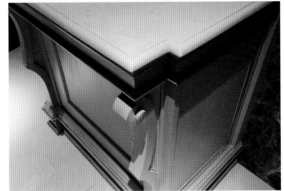

Master bathroom clad in very large panels of Emperador Dark.
The floor is covered with Crema Marfil.

A Boffi kitchen with a work surface and
floor in white Carrara marble.

The boys' bathroom in masculine and yet warm colours of Macchia Vecchia, white Lasa marble and yellow Troye.

**P.94**

In the master bathroom in this manor designed by Themenos, Van den Weghe - The Stonecompany realised the custom-made work in Fior di Bosco with lots of moulding combined with a parquet floor.

The Alhambra of the Low Countries!
In the cellar a wellness room was clad in Moroccan zeliges and Golden Brown as the main marble.
Golden Brown was also chosen for around the Jacuzzi (realised by Antheunis).
The hewn vase and fountain are realised in Bianco Statuario.

# A LUXURIOUS

## AND REFINED RETREAT

T his project is the result of the good cooperation between the owners (passionate art collectors) and interior architect Guillaume Da Silva, who took on the complete restoration of this well situated Brussels town house (450 m² living area).

The aim was to expose the original architecture and to restore it authentically. The small rooms were preserved in this and transformed into intimate, pleasant living spaces.

This interior, designed as a curiosity cabinet, stages the objects and artworks of the owners thanks to an ingenious play on perspectives, materials and a sophisticated play on light. Striving for refinements in this way ensures a harmonious and comfortable, luxurious feeling that fits completely in the lifestyle and expectations of the owners.

The entrance hall with its majestic stairs is the true backbone of this home that extends over three storeys. "Medusa" chandeliers from Baxter, wall paper by Arte.

The original tiling and wood panelling in the entrance hall were restored in detail.

The dining room is an intimate space that comes into its full splendour in the evening, in the candlelight of dinners where refinement and conviviality go hand in hand.

As in every realisation by Guillaume Da Silva the kitchen is also of primordial importance here: a place where meals are prepared but also a place for exchanges and tasting.
The central La Cornue cooking island structures the room and provides axes.
The custom-made parts, designed by Guillaume Da Silva, are clad in glossy red lacquer.
A painting by Chantal Maskens.
The kitchen work surface and the floor were covered in natural stone from Vinalmont.

The living room on the first floor with a fireplace covered with mother of pearl like a jewel. The stucco plaster ceilings and parquet floor were fully restored.

The library is an intimate place, literally a curiosity cabinet where there is lots of space to store the many books and objects.

The master bathroom is a masculine room. A single material (black glass mosaic from Bisazza) for the floors, walls and the furniture creates power and simplicity in this room.

The bathroom of the lady of the house is the most glamorous room.
Bisazza mosaic, Foscarini lighting and furniture designed by
Guilllaume Da Silva.

# HOME SERIES

## Volume 24 : DETAILS IN ARCHITECTURE

The reports in this book are selected from the Beta-Plus collection of home-design books: www.betaplus.com
They have been compiled in a special series by Le Figaro in French language: Ma Déco

Copyright © 2010 Beta-Plus Publishing / Le Figaro
Originally published in French language

**PUBLISHER**
Beta-Plus Publishing
Termuninck 3
B – 7850 Enghien
Belgium
www.betaplus.com
info@betaplus.com

**PHOTOGRAPHY**
Jo Pauwels

**DESIGN**
Polydem - Nathalie Binart

**TRANSLATIONS**
Txt-Ibis

ISBN : 978-90-8944-078-5

Printed in China